£5.99

Creative Director Tricia Legault
Designer Diana Legault Craft
Editorial Director Guy Davis
Managing Editor Linda Dowdy
Editor Gayla Amaral
Contributing Illustrators Darren McKee, Chris Sharp, Robert Alvord

Published by
Pedigree Books Limited
The Old Rectory
Matford Lane
Exeter EX2 4PS

©2000 Lyons Partnership, L.P. All rights reserved. The names and characters Barney, Baby Bop and BJ and the Barney and star and overlapping dino spots logos are trademarks of the Lyons Partnership, L.P. Barney, BJ and the Barney and star logo are Reg. U.S. Pat. & Tm. Off.

Contents

Barney's Adventure Map..6
Barney's Outer Space Adventure.....................................8
The Rocket Song...29
Barney's Rocket Ship Adventure Maze...........................30
Astronaut Dress-Up..32
Astronaut Match-Up...33
A Is For Astronaut..34
Let's Make A Rocket Ship..35
Barney On Safari..36
Jungle Maze...42
Jungle Animal Match-Up...43
Circus Search & Spot..44
Treasure Island Search & Spot......................................46
Undersea Search & Spot...48
Fishing Song..50
Sand Search..52
S Is For Sand...53
Camping Search & Spot..54
Crazy Camp Mix-Up..56
A-Camping We Will Go!...57
Who's Awake?..61

Barney's Adventure Map

Join Barney and his friends, BJ and Baby Bop, as they share one adventure after another. From a treasure island to outer space to a jungle safari, Barney discovers adventure everywhere his imagination takes him!

Barney's Outer Space Adventure

Written by Mark S. Bernthal • Illustrated by Robert Alvord

One starry night, Barney and Baby Bop look up at the sky through a telescope.

Suddenly, Baby Bop shouts excitedly, "Barney! Look what I see!"

Barney is surprised when he peeks through the telescope. "It's a little girl from another planet looking at us through her telescope!"

"I wish we could fly to her planet and visit her," says BJ.

"Oh, I imagine we can," chuckles Barney.

Suddenly, BJ's toy rocket grows bigger and bigger!

"Let's climb aboard our rocket!" says Barney.

10, 9, 8, 7, 6, 5, 4, 3, 2, 1… Blast off!
The rocket zooms into outer space towards the little girl's planet!

"Look!" says Baby Bop. "It's the cow who jumped over the moon!"

"That's right," says Barney. "And look—the man in the moon is smiling at us."

"Wow!" exclaims BJ. "I can see a real astronaut! Outer space is so exciting!"

"Welcome to the Planet Toompa!" shouts the excited little girl. "I am Meebeedeep, but you can call me Meeby!"

"Greetings!" calls Barney happily. "I'm Barney, and these are my friends, Baby Bop and BJ!"

"Are all grown-ups on your planet purple and green like Barney?" giggles Meeby.

"No," laughs BJ, "Barney is kind of special."

Meeby shows her new friends around her planet.

"Rainbows shine everywhere when light hits the Sun-Jewel Mountains," explains Meeby.

"Very pretty!" exclaims Baby Bop.

Next, they pass the Great Soda Sea.

"It's an ocean of raspberry soda that you can really drink," says Meeby.

"Can you swim in it?" asks BJ.

"Sure," giggles Meeby, "but the bubbles really tickle!"

Just then, a Bloopie fish splashes by calling out, "Bloopie! Bloopie!"

"Here's something you'll like," giggles Meeby. "On our planet, children have their very own Tickle Tree!"

The Tickle Tree makes Barney and his friends laugh and giggle for hours!

"Would you like to learn one of my favourite games?" asks Baby Bop. "It's called 'The Itsy Bitsy Spider.'"

"Whee! This is fun!" shouts Meeby excitedly.

"We have to go home now," says Barney. "Thanks for showing us your planet, Meeby!"

"Maybe you can visit us on Earth," adds BJ.

"Yes! I can't wait to see you again," says Baby Bop.

"I'll see you soon," replies Meeby. "Fly home safely!"

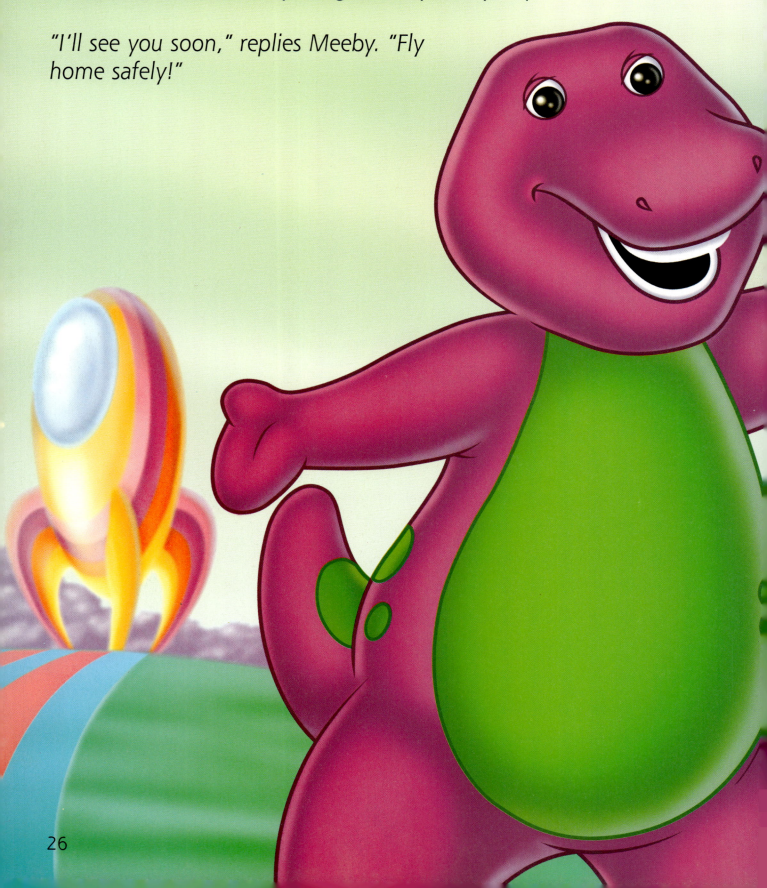

Baby Bop waves good night to Meeby through her telescope.

"Something special happened today," says Barney. "We made a new friend! And it's fun to keep in touch with friends, even if they live far, far away!"

THE ROCKET SONG

Music - Traditional
Lyrics by Stephen Bates Baltes

FIVE!
FOUR!
THREE!
TWO!
ONE!
BLAST OFF!

Flying high in the sky,
We look back and
    wave good-bye,
As our spaceship is flying away.

Past the Earth and the stars,
Look, there's Jupiter and Mars,
As our spaceship is flying away.

For it's 1-2-3,
Lots of fun for you and me.
Barney's the captain
    of the day – Hooray!

When he leads the way
Everything is A-OK,
As our spaceship is flying away.
Hip-hooray!

Flying high in the sky,
We look back and
    wave good-bye,
As our spaceship is flying away.

Past the Earth and the stars,
Look, there's Jupiter and Mars,
As our spaceship is flying away.

For it's 1-2-3,
Lots of fun for you and me.
Barney's the captain
    of the day – Hooray!

When he leads the way
Everything is A-OK,
As our spaceship is flying away.
Hip-hooray!

©1990 Shimbaree Music (ASCAP)

Astronaut Dress-Up

Astronaut Barney is getting ready for an adventure in outer space. Can you find the things Barney might need?

Astronaut Match-UP

Astronauts wear special space helmets. Barney, BJ, and Baby Bop made helmets to wear in their rocket ship. Can you find the matching helmets? How do you know to whom each helmet belongs?

Astronaut Activity

Your child can have fun making a space helmet. Provide a paper carrier bag and markers, crayons, and assorted odds and ends for decorating. Encourage your child's creativity and imagination. It's so much fun, you may want to make a helmet for yourself! When your helmets are ready, where will you go?

A is for Astronaut

The word astronaut begins with the letter A.
What other things can you find in this picture
that begin with A?

Let's Make A Rocket Ship

1. You will need: a big box, a large piece of poster board, markers and paints, and a grown-up.

2. Ask a grown-up to help. Cut a door and windows in the box. Cut a big half-circle from the poster board, form it into a cone, and tape it. Cut fins from the box flaps. Tape all the pieces together.

3. Decorate your rocket ship with paints and markers. Use your imagination!

4. Have fun in your rocket ship. Where will you go?

Illustration by Dara Goldman

Barney On Safari

Vroom! Vroom! Vroom!

Barney's on his way to a jungle adventure. Which of these animals can be found in the jungle?
elephant, chicken, giraffe, cow, horse, monkey, lion, sheep

Roar! Roar! Roar!

Barney meets the 'King of the Jungle!'
Can you roar like a lion?

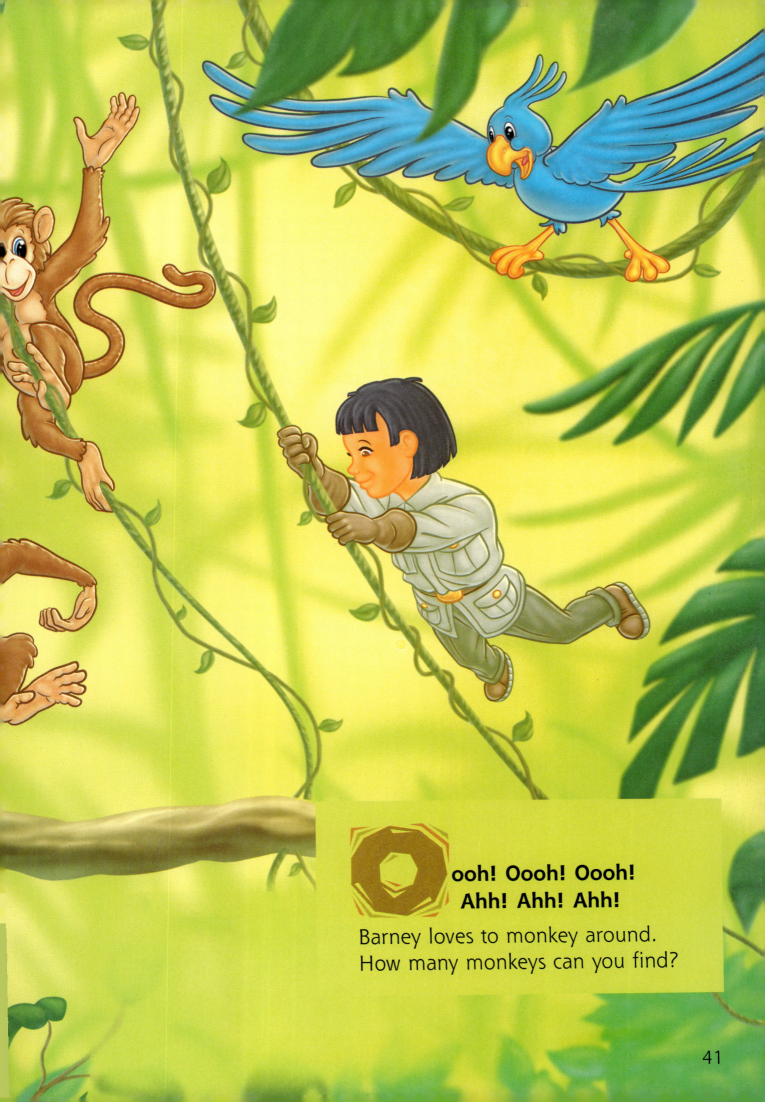

Jungle Maze

Barney's lost in the jungle. Can you help him find the way to his jungle treehouse?

Jungle Animal Match-Up

Barney's jungle animal friends are looking for their shadows. Can you help each one find his shadow?

Illustrations by Darren McKee

Circus Search & Spot

Barney's circus train
Brings fun to your town,
With lions and monkeys
And a really tall clown!

Can you find these things?

elephant

flag

seal

umbrella

monkey

Treasure Island Search & Spot

On Barney's big ship
He sails the high seas!
Can you find the treasure?
Look closely – you'll see!

treasure chest

sea shell

note in a bottle

toucan

turtle

Undersea Search & Spot

Barney goes underwater
In his big purple sub!
There's so much to see
Down under – glub! glub!

Can you find these things?

octopus

anchor

shark

starfish

angelfish

Fishing Song

Barney and Baby Bop like to go fishing in the summer.
You can join them! Just use your imagination
and sing one of Barney's favourite songs.
Can you find nine fish in this picture?

Music and Lyrics: Traditional

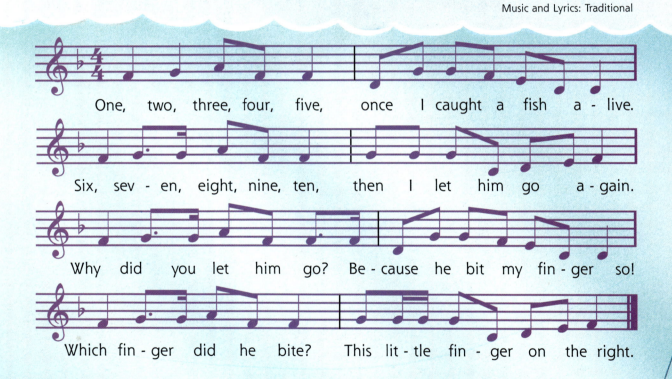

One, two, three, four, five, once I caught a fish a-live.
Six, sev-en, eight, nine, ten, then I let him go a-gain.
Why did you let him go? Be-cause he bit my fin-ger so!
Which fin-ger did he bite? This lit-tle fin-ger on the right.

Sand Search

Barney is playing hide-and-seek with his friends. Can you find who made each path in the sand?

Camping Search & Spot

Barney and his friends are going on a camping trip. Can you help BJ and Baby Bop find these things in the forest?

bear

bunny

butterfly

flowers

berries

Crazy Camp Mix-UP

When the dinos reach camp, Barney discovers his two little dino-pals have packed a few extra items. Can you find the items that don't belong on a camping trip?

Crazy Camp Mix-Up answers: bookshelf, lamp, clock, skates, octopus, television, elephant, tricycle, piano, toaster, penguin, bird cage

A-Camping We Will Go!

One summer day, Barney, BJ and Baby Bop went camping. Barney packed the tent and sleeping bags. BJ packed the hot dogs and a torch. Baby Bop got her pillow and her blankey. Everyone helped.

Written by Margie Larsen   Illustrations by June Valentine-Ruppe

After the tent was set up, the sun went down and the sky darkened. The night sky was full of stars. "What will we do now?" asked Baby Bop. Barney counted the stars, BJ chased fireflies, and Baby Bop... where was Baby Bop?

Baby Bop was fast asleep with her soft pillow and her snuggly blankey. Camping was lots of work and lots of fun too!

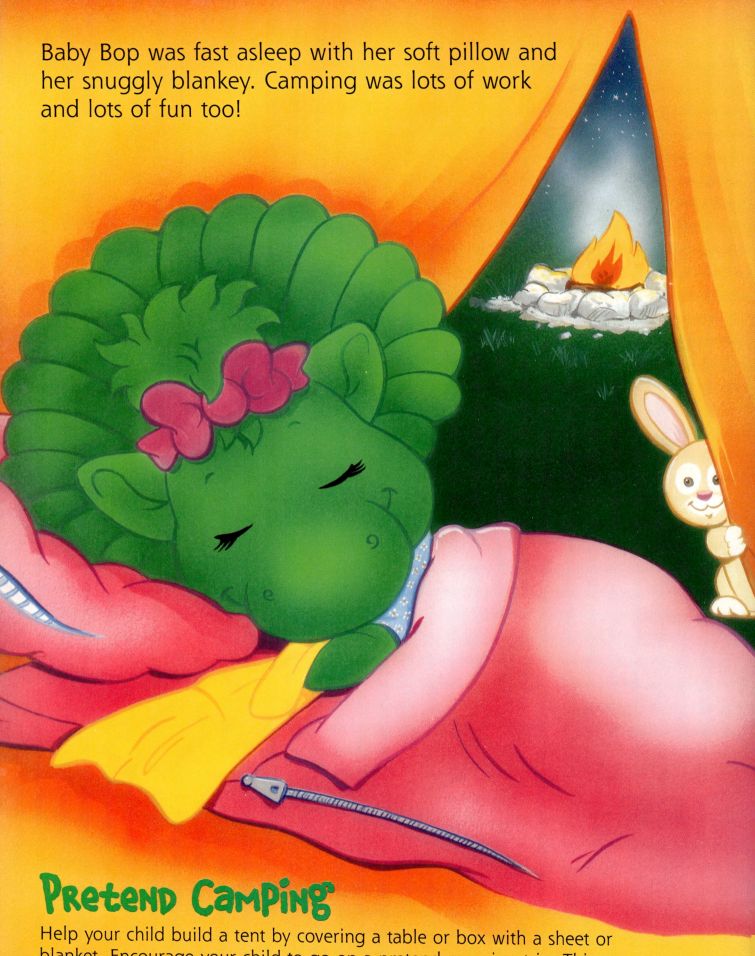

Pretend Camping

Help your child build a tent by covering a table or box with a sheet or blanket. Encourage your child to go on a pretend camping trip. Things you might include: torch, play food for a cookout, small blocks or sticks for a campfire, a pillow and a sleeping bag.

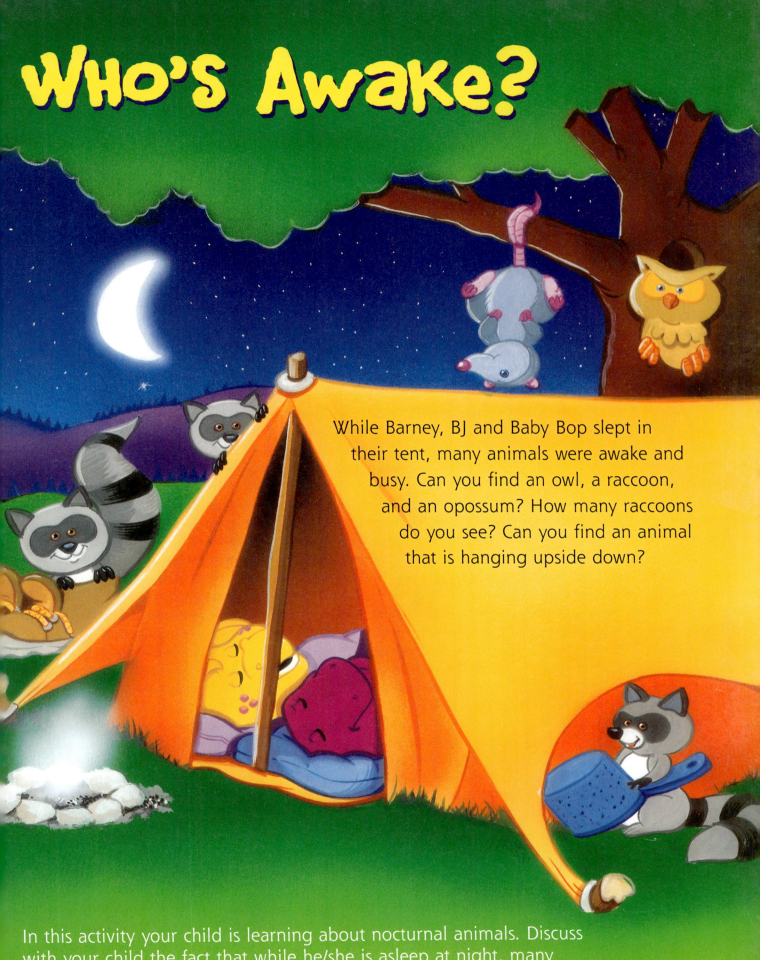

Who's Awake?

While Barney, BJ and Baby Bop slept in their tent, many animals were awake and busy. Can you find an owl, a raccoon, and an opossum? How many raccoons do you see? Can you find an animal that is hanging upside down?

In this activity your child is learning about nocturnal animals. Discuss with your child the fact that while he/she is asleep at night, many animals are busy working. Go outside at night with your child and have him/her look and listen for animal sounds. What sounds can you hear?